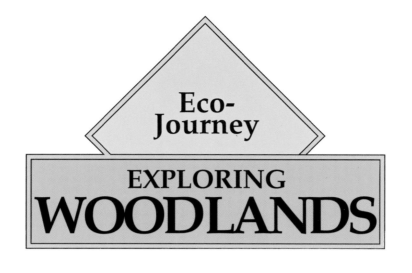

Eco-Journey

EXPLORING
WOODLANDS

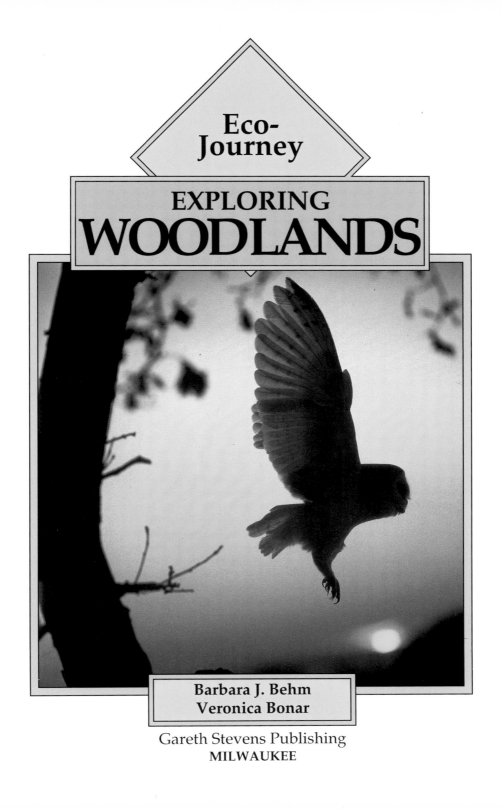

Eco-Journey

EXPLORING
WOODLANDS

Barbara J. Behm
Veronica Bonar

Gareth Stevens Publishing
MILWAUKEE

For a free color catalog describing Gareth Stevens' list of high-quality books, call 1-800-341-3569 (USA) or 1-800-461-9120 (Canada).

ISBN 0-8368-1068-6

North American edition first published in 1994 by
Gareth Stevens Publishing
1555 North RiverCenter Drive, Suite 201
Milwaukee, WI 53212, USA

This edition © 1994 by Zoë Books Limited. First produced as *Take a Square of Woodland* © 1992 by Zoë Books Limited, original text © 1992 by Veronica Bonar. Additional end matter © 1994 by Gareth Stevens, Inc. Published in the USA by arrangement with Zoë Books Limited, Winchester, England.

Photographic acknowledgments
The publishers wish to acknowledge, with thanks, the following photographic sources:
t = top *b* = bottom
Cover: J. S. Gifford/NHPA; Title page: Bruce Coleman Ltd.; pp. 6 Stephen Dalton/NHPA; 7, 8*t* E. A. Janes/NHPA; 8*b* J. & M. Bain/NHPA; 9, 10*t*, 10*b*, 11, 12*t* Bruce Coleman Ltd., 12*b* Melvin Grey/ NHPA; 13, 14, 15*t*, 15*b*, 16*t*, 16*b*, 17, 18 Bruce Coleman Ltd.; 19*t* Melvin Grey/NHPA; 19*b* N. Dennis/ NHPA; 20*t*, 20*b*, 21 Bruce Coleman Ltd.; 22 Stephen Dalton/NHPA; 23*t*, 23*b*, 24, 25*t*, 25*b*, 26, 27*t* Bruce Coleman Ltd.; 27*b* Laurie Campbell/NHPA.

Printed in the United States of America

1 2 3 4 5 6 7 8 9 99 98 97 96 95 94

Title page:
A barn owl flies silently through the woods
in search of its prey.

Contents

Words that appear in the glossary are printed in **boldface** type the first time they occur in the text.

This is the woodland

Unlike a forest, a woodland contains more than trees. Tall trees form the **canopy layer** of a woodland. Shrubs and short trees form the **shrub layer.** Other, smaller plants form

▶ Moss and ferns grow in the herb layer of this woodland along a stream.

In autumn, the leaves of these beech trees change color. Then the leaves dry up and fall off. Earthworms, woodlice, and millipedes eat the dead and decaying leaves.

the **herb layer**. Trees that lose their leaves in the fall are **deciduous** trees. Their leaves fall off because there is less light then for the leaves to make food.

The woodland in spring

▶ Bluebells create a bright carpet of color in early spring.

▼ The buds on a sycamore tree open in late March. The scent of the flowers attracts bees and other insects that drink the flowers' nectar.

Plants in the herb layer flower in spring before the trees above block the light. The first insects appear on calm, sunny days.

Queen bumblebees zigzag back and forth looking for nesting places.

◄ In spring, a female owl will lay one egg at a time in her nest. She sits on the first one for two days before she lays the second. The first owlet is several days old when the last one hatches.

Damp and decay

Most of the year, the woodland floor is damp. Tree roots hold moisture in the soil, and the leaves block the light.

▲ Woodlice live in damp, dark places such as rotting wood. They come out only at night.

▶ These male stag beetles are fighting. The stronger beetle seizes the other in his large jaws and will toss him to the ground. The winner will mate with the female beetle.

10

◀ This fungus lives on oak and elder trees. It can grow up to 4 inches (10 centimeters) across.

A **fungus** is a plant that cannot make its own food. It feeds on other plants.

On the ground

The herb layer is home to many different kinds of animals – pheasants, badgers, foxes, rabbits, shrews, voles, beetles, spiders, earthworms, grubs, and many more.

▲ This young monarch butterfly is drying its wings in the sun.

▶ The female woodcock uses dry leaves to make a nest on the woodland floor. The coloring and markings on the backs of the chicks help keep them hidden.

◄ These young foxes, called kits, live in an underground den with their mother. When they are about four weeks old, they will begin to play outside the den.

All these animals make different **food webs**. They eat certain animals, and certain animals eat them. Each animal in the web is a source of food for the next.

Under the ground

Wireworms, springtails, and bristletails live under the woodland floor. They need damp soil to keep their bodies moist. Moles,

▶ Wood ants live together in a large nest that they build from leaves and twigs. Sometimes the ants find a dead insect, such as a butterfly. They drag this food back to their nest.

◀ This bank vole has collected a pile of hawthorn berries to eat in its underground nest.

▼ Moles use their front paws as shovels to dig a network of underground tunnels.

badgers, mice, voles, and foxes also live under the woodland floor. Snails spend the winter buried in leaves. In warm weather, they crawl out to eat.

In the trees

During winter, the eggs of insects such as moths and wasps lie hidden under tree bark. The eggs hatch in spring.

▲ An adult woodpecker grips the bark of a tree with its claws and supports itself with its stiff tail feathers in order to feed its young.

▶ A cuckoo laid an egg in a hedge sparrow's nest, and the sparrow must feed the youngster.

16

◀ Some snail shells are pale yellow, and others have bold, brown stripes. The white-lipped snail in this picture (left) has various colors and patterns.

Female birds lay their eggs in nests in trees. Squirrels run along the branches of the trees of the canopy layer. Moths rest, **camouflaged**, on the trees.

After dark

Many woodland animals, such as spiders, snails, and slugs, come out only after dark so they can remain hidden from enemies.

▶ A female glowworm lights up at night. The light at the end of her body attracts the male glowworm.

◀ Like all other owls, this tawny owl has very good hearing. It can hear the smallest rustle of a mouse on the ground. It swoops down silently to catch the mouse.

Most owls rest during the day and hunt for mice and other prey at night. An owl can twist its head completely around to see what is behind it.

▼ Before a badger leaves its home at night to hunt, it sniffs the air to make sure there is no danger.

Summer plenty

▶ This large copper butterfly spreads its wings and warms its body in the sun.

▼ The flowers on this bilberry bush are pollinated by bees. As a result, the bush will grow juicy, blue-black berries.

In summer, bees and butterflies feed in the woodland clearings. As they feed, the insects carry **pollen** from one flower to the next. This causes seeds, berries, and other fruits to grow on the plants. Also in summer, bees build **hives**, and wasps build nests from wood mixed with saliva.

▼ Deer eat plants in the woodland. This stag's new antlers are covered with a soft, furry skin called "velvet."

Autumn color

When the weather cools, there are not many insects for birds to eat. Instead, they eat nuts and berries.

▶ The red cap of the fly agaric fungus is spotted with white. These colors warn animals that this fungus is poisonous.

◄ Spider webs shine with dew on damp autumn days. Spiders feed on insects that fall into the webs.

▼ Leaves change their color in autumn. They stop making food for the tree and lose their green color.

Mushrooms, molds, and mildew are known as fungi. In the autumn, many types of fungi have brilliant colors that light up the woodland floor.

Ready for winter

Tree seeds store food for new plants. In winter, many animals live on these seeds.

▶ In winter, woodmice eat stored nuts and berries. They have stored the food in empty bird nests, hollow trees, and in the ground.

24

◀ Jays bury acorns in the soil. They find the acorns again by looking for oak seedlings that grow out of the soil.

▼ A squirrel sits on a tree stump to feed. The squirrel gnaws a small hole in the nut. Then it splits the nut open.

As the weather gets colder, some birds store food in cracks in tree bark. Earthworms and beetles bury themselves deeper in the soil to keep warm.

The woodland in winter

Some animals **hibernate** during winter.   Their body temperature falls, and their heartbeat slows. They use very little energy and live off stored fat.

▶ Dormice may spend more than half the year asleep. They curl up inside their nests during winter, hardly breathing, until spring comes.

◄ A wood pigeon fluffs out its feathers in the cold weather. The air that is then trapped between the feathers soon warms up. This helps keep the bird warm.

▼ A snowfall has highlighted the leafless branches of a beech tree.

After a snowfall, the woodland is cold and quiet. Birds eat any buds, berries, and insects that may be available. Some birds keep warm by huddling together.

More Books to Read

In the Woods. Ermanno Cristini and Luigi Puricelli
(Picture Book Studio)

Mousekin's Lost Woodland. Edna Miller (S & S Trade)

Trees. Sharon Gordon (Troll)

A Walk in the Woods. Caroline Arnold (Silver Press)

Woodlands. Victor Mitchell (Lion USA)

Videotapes

Call or visit your local library to see if these videotapes are available for your viewing.

The Enchanted Forest (An old hermit teaches a young boy to love the forest and its creatures.)

The Wonderful World of Disney: The Ranger of Brownstone. (with J. Audubon Woodlore and D. Duck, followed by live-action footage of birds).

Places to Write

For information on Audubon nature centers near you, contact:
National Audubon Society
700 Broadway
New York, NY 10003

For more information regarding woodlands and wildlife, contact:

U.S. Department of
   Agriculture
Forest Service
Public Affairs/Publications
Auditors Building 2 Central
201 Fourteenth Street, S.W.
Washington, D.C. 20250

Internal Ministry of
   the Environment
Public Information
First Floor
135 St. Clair Avenue, West
Toronto, Ontario M4V 1P5

Interesting Facts

1. Trees spread out their leaves so that each leaf receives sunlight to make food.

2. In spring, plants on the woodland floor grow and flower before the tree leaves above get big and shut out the sunlight.

3. In autumn, bacteria and insects break down the fallen leaves to make rich new soil.

4. Plant foods in the soil are taken in by the roots of plants.

5. Queen bumblebees often nest in mouse holes or under piles of dry leaves.

6. Woodlice have flat bodies and seven pairs of legs. They only come out at night.

7. Badgers and foxes hunt along the woodland floor at night, looking for earthworms, insects, grubs, and woodmice.

8. Wireworms, springtails, and bristletails hate light because it dries their bodies out.

9. The land snail often has one pair of short tentacles plus another, longer pair with eyes on them.

10. Snails usually shred food with their hundreds of tiny teeth located on a tonguelike organ outside of their mouths before they pull the food inside.

Glossary

camouflage: the condition that occurs when the coloring of the fur, feathers, or skin, or the shape of an animal makes the animal difficult to see against its background.

canopy layer: the covering made by the tallest trees in the woodland.

deciduous: refers to the trees that lose their leaves in autumn.

food web: the plants and animals linked together providing food for one another.

fungus: a plant that cannot make its own food.

herb layer: the plants that grow on the woodland floor beneath the shrubs.

hibernate: to spend winter in a state of rest.

hives: colonies made by bees.

pollen: tiny spores produced by plants as a fine dust.

shrub layer: the bushes and short trees in the woodland.

Index